LONDON ZOO™
CONSERVATION IN ACTION

SAVING THE ANIMALS

Written by
Kate Petty

Published in association
with London Zoo

Hodder
Children's
Books

a division of Hodder Headline plc

Published by Hodder Children's Books 1998

10 9 8 7 6 5 4 3 2 1

ISBN 0 340 71479 4

Printed by Mackays of Chatham plc, Chatham, Kent
Hodder Children's Books
A Division of Hodder Headline plc
338 Euston Road
London NW1 3BH

CONTENTS

* Explanation of words in **bold** type in the book

FOREWORD

The good modern zoo is an amazing place —
far removed from the Victorian-style
menagerie that used to exist almost
everywhere, and still does in many places.

In the new-style zoo, conservation is the key
word, through captive breeding programmes,
through conservation work in the wild, through
scientific research into the biology of
threatened species and habitats, and through
information provided for the visitors, which we
hope will inspire them to conservation action
of their own.

London Zoo is no exception. Over the last
fifty years, and particularly in the last ten,
it has changed from being a 'collection' of
representative animal species from around the
world, to being a place where we hope nobody
can miss the fact that conservation is what
drives us on.

London Zoo is one part of the Zoological

Society of London, which also runs Whipsnade Wild Animal Park, The Institute of Zoology (a major conservation biology research institute), and many field conservation projects around the world; it is this wide combination of conservation activities that make it unique.

I hope you enjoy reading this book about the important work that we do. Please come and visit us and see 'conservation in action'.

Jo Gipps.

Director, London Zoo

SO YOU WANT TO BE A ZOO-KEEPER?

There are about sixty keepers at London Zoo, with 5000 **vertebrates** and 12,000 **invertebrates** to look after. If you've ever had a pet of your own you will know that caring for animals is mostly about cleaning out where they live, and giving regular feeding and plenty of companionship. Zoo-keepers grow fond of their animals but *petting* them is not on the agenda. The animals must be left to lead their animal lives – they are part of a **conservation** project – definitely not pets. **Hand-rearing** is undertaken only as a last resort.

A keeper's day starts early – at 8am – and finishes when the Zoo closes for the night. Once the animals have been checked in the mornings, their enclosures must be mucked out and their food prepared. Good keepers understand their animals very well and know quickly if something is wrong.

New keepers spend two years studying for a Certificate in Animal Management and learning practical skills in observing and caring for animals and keeping good records of what they see. Others arrive with relevant qualifications – in Biology or Geology, for example.

It is a very rewarding job, and many of the senior keepers have been there thirty years or more. Certainly everyone I spoke to while researching this book seemed to be passionately involved in their work with the animals.

"I MET A LION TODAY"

We could hear a lion roaring – almost barking – in short, loud bursts. I was in the 'mess' room (where the keepers go to sit down, catch up on paper work, etc.) talking to head keeper Ray Charter about some of the other big cats, the Sumatran tigers. Ray nodded in the direction of the noise. "Sometimes they get so loud you can't hear yourself speak," he said. "This is nothing."

The roars got louder. "It sounds very close," I said nervously.
"It is," he said.
"So where are they?" I asked.
"Just next door. Would you like to take a look?"

I'd never met a lion before, so I said yes. Ray opened a door and there, behind two sets of stout fencing, was a beautiful golden lion with a thick coat and mane. I was impressed.

The lion knew Ray and started to show off, roaring and scampering about, a bit like a kitten. But this was no kitten.

"Would you like to get closer?" Ray asked. "OK," I said, feeling that I was about to take my life in my hands, and he took us through a gate to the next fence. I was within touching distance. The lion was smaller at close quarters than I'd imagined, about waist height. He leant against the barrier that separated us, rubbing his lovely fur against the mesh fence like a cat rubbing against your legs. I kept my hands firmly in my pockets, but I longed to stroke him. Ray must have known.

"Put your hands through that fence and he'd have your fingers off quick as a flash," he warned. I buried my hands deeper still in my pockets.

The lion became positively skittish, racing from end to end of the narrow space behind the fence. "He's getting a bit worked up now," said Ray. "He really wants all my attention. We'd better go back and let him calm down. We're pretty safe here but I think we'll leave him."

Only pretty safe? Don't want to rush or anything . . . I must admit I was quite keen to get back to the other side of the door!

But what a treat! I kept saying to myself, "I met a lion today." And it wasn't just any old lion. It was Kamal, an Asian lion (and I'd always thought all lions lived in Africa), one of only 400 left on the planet. Asian lions were the ones that were fed a **diet** of Christians in Roman times. Their manes are less developed than an African lion's and they have an extra fold of skin on the abdomen.

The few remaining wild Asian lions all live in the Gir Forest in north-west India, though long ago they roamed throughout the Middle East and northern India. London Zoo's Asian lions are part of a **captive breeding** programme and are doing well. In fact, there were three half-grown cubs outside on the terraces with their mother Ruchi. Ruchi is very protective and has had no problems rearing her cubs herself. They were fathered by Jake, now returned to his home in Chester Zoo. Kamal is housed next door to Ruchi, because although male lions are very tolerant of their own cubs, they will usually kill another lion's cubs. So Kamal, who is still quite young himself, must wait until the cubs have grown up before he can be a mate for Ruchi.

Captive breeding ensures that a **species** does not become **extinct** and only works as part of a wider conservation programme. The lions in the Gir forest are now also protected in the wild. Local farmers receive compensation for the few cattle taken by lions, so the lions are left alone and are breeding well there. A programme has started to move some of them into a new area, one with enough greenery for cover and plenty of food.

Soon no one will be able to make my mistake of thinking that lions are only found in Africa.

CARING FOR BEARS

How do you care for bears? Real ones, that is. Twelve years ago, the famous Mappin Terraces at London Zoo were closed and the bears that lived there were sent to other zoos where there was more room for them. Some people feel that bears just do not belong in zoos. They are intelligent animals that need a lot of space and plenty to do. Older people remember seeing bears that were plainly unhappy, though for many zoo visitors bears are the most popular animals.

They are also all species threatened to varying degrees. One way and another, humans have reduced their numbers to danger level. They have been hunted, captured as pets, made to dance and perform, cruelly baited and cut up to be used as medicine, as well as losing their **habitat** to human settlements. Until 700 years ago there were bears even in Britain. Now there are brown bears in very few places outside Russia and Canada. Most at risk are the three sorts of smaller bears that live in Asia – sloth bears, Asiatic black bears, and sun bears – and giant pandas. There are probably less than 8000 sloth bears left in the world.

Recently the man-made mountains of the Mappin Terraces were refurbished. The 13 different enclosures were made into one huge one, the largest bear enclosure in any urban zoo in the world, with rocks and trees and grassy slopes and water for them to play in. Now all it needed was some bears.

The newcomers were a pair of sloth bears from Sri Lanka, where there are only 400 left, which came via a zoo in Poland. Sloth bears are small and furry, they have thick black hair all over except for round their noses. Their eyesight is not very good, but their sense of smell is excellent. Their long noses and long claws are well suited to finding and eating the insects that are their food. In the wild they suck up termites so noisily that it is said they can be heard 100 metres away! The animals had been well cared for at their previous zoo but their enclosure was being knocked down for a new building.

The sloth bears are not alone in their new 2500-square-metre home. They share it with deer (Reeve's muntjac), monkeys (Hanuman langurs), waterfowl and peacocks. The variety of creatures makes the enclosure a much more interesting place for the bears to live. The langurs were cautious of the bears at first but now they are used to them. Hanuman langurs are not a threatened species – quite the opposite, in fact. They play a part in Indian folklore and in Hindu culture they are sacred.

Bears are time-consuming animals to look after. They are intelligent and need to be kept busy. They can also be dangerous. Sloth bears are aggressive around humans: in some parts of India, people are more afraid of being attacked by a sloth bear than by a tiger.

In the wild, bears spend most of their day looking for food. They are omnivores, eating fruits, roots and leaves, as well as insects and a few small animals. The best way to keep them occupied and healthy is to make their food hard to find.

The bears are fed a varied diet that includes fruit, berries, porridge sweetened with honey, insects and coconuts. Sometimes the food is put inside a log so the bears have to find a way of getting it out. Food is often put in awkward places so as to make the bears use their intelligence to get at it. But even random feeding times and hidden food is not enough. Keeper Malcolm Fitzpatrick has to work hard to keep the bear enclosure interesting with plenty of **'behavioural**

enrichment' for them. New objects are put into the enclosure all the time so that the bears can sniff them and explore them and exercise their curiosity to keep them active mentally.

The male sloth bear has a friendly personality and seems happy with his stimulating environment. The female on the other hand is much more difficult to deal with. She swings her head, which is one of the few bear signs of distress, and tends to stay near doorways (a habit she developed in her previous home). She gets agitated when there are too many people around. She probably associates the doorways with the arrival of food and people with the possibility of more food being thrown to her. The keepers have tried everything to make her better, including boarding up the doorways and making some areas inaccessible to the public. She probably just needs a longer time to settle.

Meanwhile it is possible that something else might change her behaviour and keep her occupied. The sloth bear pair produced cubs in their previous home and they have been seen mating since they arrived in their new one. It is likely that she is pregnant.

Unlike most bears, sloth bears don't **hibernate** in winter. A female has her cubs in early winter and they emerge from the cubbing den at Easter time. Now only time will tell whether the female has found her own 'behavioural enrichment' or whether the keepers will have to devise more and more elaborate excitements and novelties to keep the bears on their toes.

OPEN WIDE!

Harley Street, famous for its top doctors and dentists, is not far from Regent's Park where the Zoo is located. Luckily for tigers with toothache, Harley Street dentist Dr Peter Kertesz divides his time between his human patients and animals. He has built up an amazing collection of animal dentistry equipment – for treating monkeys and apes, bears and elephants as well as big cats.

Recently he went with the Tiger Support Team to treat three Amur tigers in Moscow. On another recent visit to Russia he did a giant filling for an elephant – in its tusk!

HOME FROM HOME

It would be sad if the sleepy dormouse of *Alice in Wonderland* or the chirpy crickets that you hear on warm summer evenings became simply creatures that you read about in books, and extinct in real life. You've heard about rainforests being cleared and deserts expanding, but you might not know that the British countryside is changing too. Some of our native animals also face extinction because their habitat is disappearing.

The dormouse and the field cricket are two English animals that are in danger of being lost. Lose them and we lose a bit of England for ever, because it would mean that we had lost the special sorts of countryside they live in – hedgerows and woodlands for dormice, sunny pastures for crickets. As you know, conservationists have to focus on the habitat as much as on the animal – protect the habitat and the animal has at least some chance of survival. What's more, if the habitat is looked after, the other creatures that share it also have a better chance of survival.

Dormice are cute and furry – even their tails are furry – so people want to save them. One of the good things about a conservation project for such a popular animal is that a whole range of less obviously attractive creatures (such as beetles and spiders) get saved along with them. London Zoo is working with the government conservation organisation called English Nature to stop dormice from dying out altogether.

Most people have never seen a dormouse. Even if you go to the Zoo where there are at least three pairs, you will probably never see one. This is because dormice are **nocturnal** animals that sleep all day. Their bodies become 'torpid', which means that all their functions slow down. If you find a dormouse in this state it has probably rolled out of its nest without even realising it. Not only are dormice nocturnal, but they hibernate from autumn until spring as well. No wonder the dormouse has a reputation for being sleepy! Even the name 'dormouse' comes from the French word *dormir* meaning 'to sleep'.

The dormouse comes somewhere between a mouse and a squirrel in the animal kingdom. Similar creatures were around 40-60 million years ago (the dinosaur age came to an end 65 million years ago). They are orangey-brown, similar to a fox in colour, and tiny – no more than 6cm in body-length. The unusual bushy tail adds a further 3cm. Even fully grown dormice weigh little more than 25g (one ounce).

Dormice rarely come down to the ground from the trees and hedgerows. Their favourite habitat is a hazel coppice, a dense growth of trees that is regularly cut back.

Coppices were common in the countryside until recently, with woodmen cutting back the trees and bushes for firewood. Now woodland is managed differently and coppicing (cutting back) is less common. But cutting back too far is worse than no cutting at all. Dormice need variety – a network of branches to live in, but not so thick that the sun can't get through to ripen the fruits and berries. Hedgerows have disappeared at an alarming rate in recent years, which is also bad news for the dormouse. The hedgerows are like highways between different bits of woodland. Without these hedgerow highways dormice get cut off in their own little patch, which is a problem when it comes to trying to find a mate from another part of the wood.

The dormice weave hedgerow nests, often from honeysuckle bark, where they sleep curled up during the day with their tails over their faces. Nursery nests to rear their young are built closer to the ground.

They make their winter nests away from the bare branches, hidden at ground level or even underground.

Unlike some other rodents that eat grass and leaves, common dormice (sometimes known as hazel dormice) need a wide and changing variety of food throughout the year. Their diet includes fruit, flowers, seeds, buds, tender bark, nuts and even insects and birds' eggs. As summer passes, the dormice eat and eat. They need to increase their weight to 30g (and no less than 20g) to survive hibernation.

They curl up in their winter nests and their heart rate and breathing slow right down. If the weather grows warmer they might surface to eat a few nuts and then go back to sleep again. When spring arrives in earnest the dormice emerge fully and the female builds a nursery nest. She may have several litters of four or five young in a year. Although the babies are blind and helpless at birth, by six weeks they are able to leave the nest and go off on their own.

So what can conservationists do? Landowners – and that includes gardeners in the country – can make sure they don't get rid of the sort of woods and hedgerows that suit dormice. The conservation scheme with English Nature concentrates on breeding dormice and putting them back in places where they used to be plentiful.

This is how it works. Once conservationists are fairly sure that dormice live in an area (you can often tell by the hazelnut shells they leave behind) they can help them by putting up a number of nesting boxes. These are similar to bird nesting boxes except that the opening faces inwards to the tree or hedge. They provide extra sheltered nests where the habitat is not as good as it was.

Dormice are a **protected species** so it is illegal for anyone to touch them, let alone take a pair from the wild. They would face a £2000 fine if they did. But if conservation workers find a late litter in a nest box – young dormice that will never be able to put on enough weight to take them through the winter hibernation – they can get permission to rescue them and take them to a zoo to breed in captivity. The babies that are born in captivity can go to other zoos or they can go back into the wild.

Releasing captive-bred animals into the wild is never a simple business, but the dormouse scheme seems to work. The release is carefully timed so that there is plenty of food around. At least twenty dormice need to be released together for them to survive. These will come from various members of the Common Dormouse Captive Breeding Group and they must all be healthy. First they are taken to a secret site. This is so no one disturbs the dormice while they are adjusting to their new environment.

Release boxes, like nesting boxes, are
attached to a tree. For a while the animals
are fed on the sort of food they're going to
have to find in the wild. Then the doors
are opened and the dormice eventually
make their own way out into the
woodland. They are checked and fed if
necessary for a little while longer. Before
they set out completely on their own they
are **tagged**, either with a little ear tattoo
or with a microchip (even tiny mouse-sized
radio collars have been tried) so that their
progress can be tracked. In this way
dormice are returning to areas where they
had all but disappeared.

In 1991 there was only one colony of
British field crickets left in Britain.
Although there are field crickets all over
Europe, the British ones, which have
adapted to the colder climate, have always
been fairly rare. These crickets are related
to grasshoppers, but you'll see them
walking along with the occasional hop
rather than leaping or even flying. The

males 'sing' to their mates by rubbing their wings together to make that characteristic chirping sound. It is this noise that gives them their name, from the French *criquer*, 'to creak'.

English Nature realized that they would have to act quickly if they were to save British field crickets from extinction. They needed to protect the surviving colony and find suitable new sites where captive-bred crickets could be introduced. In 1992 six males and six females were taken from the wild to breed at the Invertebrate Conservation Centre at London Zoo. Three months later 700 crickets were ready to be released.

Field crickets need a sheltered sunny position and short grass. New sites have been found on land where grazing sheep — or rabbits — keep the grass short. Now crickets are being put back in parts of the country where they had disappeared. Crickets have been a part of British life for many years – the naturalist Thomas Moffat referred to them in a book as long ago as 1658 – and should now continue to be so for many years to come. Incidentally, Thomas Moffat's interest in creepy-crawlies was probably not shared by his daughter, a certain "Little Miss Muffet". . .

RAINFOREST STORY

This is a rainforest story that makes you feel hopeful, I promise. After all, the well known statistics of rainforest destruction are mostly very depressing. Here are some of them: the **rainforests** survived unchanged for 60 million years until the second half of this century. By 1980, nearly half of them had been destroyed. Every minute 60 football pitches' worth of forest is lost. Burning the trees of the forest releases carbon dioxide, a so-called greenhouse gas, into the air and increases the effects of global warming.

The **tropical** rainforests, while occupying only 7% of the Earth's surface, are home to 50% of its species. You might think that maybe they could afford to lose one or two – until you saw some of the animals themselves. So let's meet some little South American monkeys, the lion tamarins, at one time predicted to be extinct by the year 2000, and see why conservationists are so passionate about saving them and the forest they live in.

Tamarins are monkeys – 'new world' monkeys of the Americas as opposed to 'old world' monkeys of Africa and Asia. Our hero, the lion tamarin – *Leontopithecus* – is particularly attractive. There are four kinds of lion tamarin and they all live in the Atlantic forest regions of Brazil. They are about the size of small cats, with beautiful long silky hair and expressive little faces. They are **primates**, like us, and it's easy to see that they are intelligent and sensitive. They live amongst the branches in the middle of the forest canopy, so they have to watch out for birds of prey from above as well as predators on the ground below. Lion tamarins live in family groups, so there are more pairs of eyes to look out for each other. Parents usually bond for life. The mother gives birth to twins roughly every eight months and the father helps to care for them. In the wild it is quite likely that one of the twins will not survive. The young males leave the family at about two years old and females about a year later.

Lion tamarins are well adapted to their tree-dwelling life, finding all their food in the trees and communicating with one another by 'singing' so that they can hear other members of the family even if they can't see them through the thick foliage. However, they don't cross water or treeless areas, which means that groups can easily become separated when trees are cut down. Unfortunately, the part of the forest that is home to the lion tamarins is also home to the densest population of humans and industrial development in Brazil. In fact, a massive 98% of the original forest has now disappeared. It seemed until recently that these delightful little primates were doomed, along with thousands of other creatures that were part of the same **'web of life'** in the rainforest. As if losing their habitat wasn't bad enough, lion tamarins were also poached for the laboratory and pet trades.

Twenty-five years ago conservationists could see that one particular lion tamarin, the golden lion tamarin, was a species in danger. A big conference was held in the United States where it was decided that it might be possible to save golden lion tamarins from extinction if a large number of countries worked together. Part of the plan was to increase the numbers of golden lion tamarins by breeding them in captivity. By 1989 the numbers of captive golden lion tamarins had risen from 70 to 500. The conservationists then had to try to find ways of saving the habitat as well as the animals themselves. Then, just as lion tamarins were hitting the headlines in 1989, a fourth species was discovered. Now, as well as golden lion tamarins, golden-headed lion tamarins and golden-rumped lion tamarins (both with black bodies), there was the black-faced lion tamarin. All four were **endangered** in the wild, though the threats they faced were different.

By 1990 it became obvious that lion tamarins in the wild were not going to survive without more help. There is a computer program called VORTEX which can predict the survival or extinction of a species if the program is fed with detailed figures about their lives, deaths and breeding habits. VORTEX is a **simulation program**. It is called a 'stochastic' simulation because it has a random factor built into it.

The random factor allows for the very likely possibility of some sort of catastrophe occurring. The results of the simulation showed that the lion tamarins were heading for extinction.

It was time for a major meeting of experts from all over the world to decide what could be done. So conservationists gathered in Brazil, the home of the lion tamarins, to pool their knowledge and draw up some guidelines. They came up with a general plan for the four sorts of lion tamarin, though each had a separate plan as well.

1. Expand the habitat (by buying up land) and protect it.

2. Make a record of all the wild lion tamarin populations and make sure they are protected.

3. Carry on with the international captive breeding programme.

4. **Reintroduce** captive-bred animals into the wild, making sure that they don't carry any diseases.

Buying land needs money. Protecting wild animals means persuading local governments and farmers that it is worth their while to do so — you can't expect people to change their lives for the sake of some animals unless there is a pay-off for them. So money and cooperation are very important in any conservation project. But if local people can be persuaded to help, and wealthy countries can be persuaded to find money, then the chances of a project succeeding are good. In the following years a huge amount of hard work and patience have improved the chances of the lion tamarins surviving into the next century.

So where does London Zoo come in? This is a case where the Zoo has been happy to play an important part in an international operation, with funding and captive breeding of golden lion tamarins, without taking the leading role. Though none of their golden lion tamarins have been re-introduced into the wild yet, they might be in the future.

What happens when animals go from captivity into the wild? Does it work? It is almost impossible that some animals will ever be able to go back, perhaps because there is nowhere to go back to or because it is hard to find a way to reintroduce them gradually. But golden lion tamarins have now been reintroduced for several years, and it seems as if it works for them. This is how it's done. A strong and healthy lion tamarin that has been bred in captivity (remember that these days they live as natural a life as possible, without human intervention, in zoos) is brought to live in a centre in Brazil. It is given time to get used to the climate and to eat the sort of foods, put there by the keepers, that it will find in the wild. A single tamarin (not one from a group) is found in the wild to be its mate and brought to share its cage. The keepers watch them carefully to make sure that they make friends, although they are often aggressive to each other at first. Once they are friends they are taken together to a protected place in the reserve. The wild one can teach the captive one where to find the food. When they are both ready to fend for themselves, they are given a thorough health check and tagged and colour coded so that their progress can be followed. So far about 200 have been reintroduced in this way and they are doing fine. In the last five years some of the couples have started to have babies, which means that the wild population might eventually start to get bigger, and maybe the target of 2000 animals by the year 2025 might even be a possibility.

FRIEDA THE FRIENDLY SPIDER

A friendly spider? One that you can stroke? Yes, that's Frieda, the Mexican red-kneed bird-eating spider. She is the size of a hamster and almost as furry. In fact, given the chance, as I was, it's hard to resist stroking her silky legs.

Frieda must be one of the world's only working spiders. London Zoo runs courses for people who have a fear of spiders – **arachnophobia**. At the end of an afternoon's course nearly all the participants are cured sufficiently to be able to stroke Frieda and have their photograph taken with her. And because the little spiders we see every day are so titchy in comparison, the former arachnophobes are also able to go home and chuck a spider out of the back door if it gets in their way, without hurting it and without screaming.

Frieda is good at her job because she doesn't move much. In fact, that's part of her attractive personality! A *spider* with a personality? It seems that, as with all animals if you spend time with a group of them, you start to be able to tell them apart. And compared with the other inhabitants of the invertebrate house, a spider will spend a long time with a keeper. Frieda and some of the other females are twenty years old! (Few other invertebrates – and that includes male spiders – live for more than a year.) So there's Lucy and Victoria (Vicky for short), Kirsty and Debbie, Charlotte and Tracy, and until recently there was the late, lamented and sadly missed Belinda, who died aged at least 22.

Frieda is docile and doesn't mind at all when Dave Clarke (Head Keeper) picks her up, but Lucy is more mobile and sometimes runs about, which doesn't go

down too well with the arachnophobes.
And Vicky is actually rather bad-tempered;
she flicks hairs at the person who is trying
to pick her up. The hairs contain an
irritant, so it tends to put people off, just
as it puts off creatures that threaten her in
the wild.

But all these old ladies recognise a
competent handler when they come across
one. Dave picks the spiders up very firmly,
gently holding their legs against their sides,
and places them on the flat of his hand. I
wanted to know how he learned this
technique, because the thought of trying it
for the first time was rather alarming,
especially as large spiders are delicate
creatures that could easily die if dropped.

Dave's answer was surprising. Guess what?
He used to be arachnophobic! The first
time he held a spider like Frieda was before
he worked at the Zoo and he was terrified!
But as soon as the spider was placed on his
hand, the experience cured Dave, and he

soon learned how to handle spiders
with confidence.

One of the questions people ask Dave
most often when he is showing them a
spider is "Can it bite?": to which his reply
is, "Can you?" Just because it can bite
doesn't mean to say it will. Most spiders
are not aggressive unless threatened.
What's more, a spider sitting on someone's
hand thinks it is on the ground – and it's
not very likely to bite the ground, is it? And
it is fairly certain to know that you're not
going to be very tasty! If you were a large
and luscious insect you might have more
cause to be frightened. However, a big
meal can last a spider for a whole year.

Bird-eating spiders like Frieda have eight
tiny eyes and fairly poor eyesight. They get
most of their information about the world
from those silky long hairs, sensing the
vibrations that are carried on the air. But if
they're feeling flirtatious, the senses they
rely on are relayed through the bottom of

their feet. In the Zoo, male and female spiders are kept separately. In the wild, the young males often migrate in gangs. . . a memorable sight if you come across them in Mexico. The females build silk-lined burrows for themselves, but the males are more likely to camp overnight, perhaps in a quickly-spun hammock. If the male is ready to mate he makes a special web on which to spread his sperm. He then charges up the syringe-like ends of his **pedipalps** (leg-like feelers) and taps on the door – literally – of the female's burrow. He taps in code so that she knows he is a suitor rather than her dinner!

Bird-eating spiders can have up to 700 young hatching from an egg sac. In the wild 90% of these would die before growing up into adults, but in the Zoo, where they are constantly warm and protected, most of them will survive. With such a high success rate, you might wonder why these spiders are protected under **CITES**, along with rhinos and elephants and other much-hunted animals. (CITES stands for Convention on International Trade in Endangered Species.) Although they are no longer on the '**red list**' of animals in greatest danger, the spiders suffer in the pet trade because they all too often end up with owners who just want a big hairy spider for a pet, and who do not understand how to care for them. Compared with the biggest bird-eating spiders, which have taken at least five years to reach that size, a two-year-old might seem unimpressively small. Inexperienced breeders don't know that they take so long to grow and get bored with them. Nor do they realise that they shouldn't allow all those brothers and sisters to breed with each other, not that you can tell what sex they are until they reach a decent size. Babies bred by the Zoo usually go to other zoos around the world to breed with spiders from different families.

Big hairy spiders can be glamorous of course. Belinda was a bit of a film star –

she and some of her friends appeared in
'Raiders of the Lost Ark'. But they had to
go along with a chaperone. The Head
Keeper who chaperoned the spiders to the
set of the James Bond film 'Dr No' ended
up standing in for Sean Connery when the
spider was filmed running across his chest.
Look hard when you get a chance to see
the film. . .

It's a good job the keepers can tell the
spiders apart by their personalities –
because sometimes it's hard to tell them
apart by their looks. This is especially true
when a spider moults, and **moulting** is
something that bird-eating spiders do quite
spectacularly. One day a spider is dull and
bald and the next she is brightly-coloured
with beautiful new soft fur. Beside her is
what looks like another spider but is in
fact the exoskeleton she has shed, furry
legs and all. You can see exactly where all
the body parts fit, and most extraordinary,
you can see the light shining into all
eight eyeholes!

Bird-eating spiders lie on their backs to moult. Unfortunately, inexperienced owners sometimes think that their pet must be dead at this point, and throw it out!

But the keeper who discovered Belinda in her box saw that although she was the right way up, her legs were curled under her – a sure sign that she was dead, after 22 years at the Zoo. Everyone was very sad when Belinda died. They felt they had lost an old friend. But her relatives live on – in their thousands.

PARROT SKETCH

People like parrots. Parrots make us laugh.
They're big, colourful, storybook birds.
And they can talk. In fact, in northern
Europe, it's hard to imagine parrots exist as
wild birds at all. It seems very peculiar to
see flocks of them flying around – if you
visit Australia, for example.

'Parrots' is a general name given to the
group of birds called 'psittaciformes'. It
includes cockatoos (they're the ones with
crests on their heads), parakeets, lories,
lorikeets, lovebirds and others. It also
includes the familiar budgerigars (there are
over three million of them in British
homes), which are little parakeets. They all
come from the southern hemisphere
where they live mostly in forests. A typical
psittaciforme is brightly coloured with a
short neck and the distinctive curved beak.
It has four toes on each foot – two facing

Asian lion cubs with one of the Zoo keepers

**An Asian lion family -
adult male and female, and cub**

Sloth bear on Bear Mountain (Mappin Terraces)

A dormouse - asleep, of course!

A cat-sized golden lion tamarin

A seahorse

A Partula snail in its tiny reserve

A Mexican Bird-eating spider, on the left, with her
recently shed, dull, exoskeleton on the right

A coati - safe on a keeper's shoulder and away from the phone!

A rare hyacinth macaw from Brazil

The lively meerkats and
graceful giraffes share an
enclosure at the Zoo.

Sumatran tiger cub, Hari, being bottle-fed

Playmates Hari and Liffey, with toys such as a ball and a dangling dustbin lid

forwards, two backwards – which it uses for gripping things. It also has a large tongue, which seems to help with 'talking', though no one is quite sure how much parrots mimic one another or 'talk' in the wild. Famous talkers are the African Grey and the Yellow-headed Amazon. Parrots are companionable birds, living in large groups but pairing for life.

One of the main reasons that parrots have become endangered species in many parts of the world is because people want them for pets. (The pet trade has also been a factor in saving some of them from total extinction. Nothing is simple in this conservation business – but more about that later.) Eggs or fledglings are stolen from their nests in the trees and transported across the world as if they were objects rather than animals. Many of them are badly treated and become bad-tempered pets – if they are not some of the 80% that die first. In some countries, such as Indonesia, it is not even illegal to

export the birds for the pet trade. In others, such as Australia, it has been illegal to export them for the last forty years. Unfortunately, there are collectors who are prepared to pay thousands and thousands of pounds for rare birds. The rarer the bird, the more money exchanges hands. A huge blue hyacinthine macaw from Brazil, though it might be trapped for food at home, can fetch £8000 abroad and it is rumoured that a collector in Saudi Arabia was offering £30,000 for a breeding pair of black cockatoos from Australia.

With so much money at stake, smugglers will go to great lengths, risking fines and imprisonment, to get rare birds to fanatical collectors. One particular gang of bird smugglers involved a whole family. The women were fitted with special bras for smuggling parrot eggs! (Just imagine if the baby parrots had decided to hatch a day or two ahead of schedule . . .) They were black cockatoo eggs taken from the wild in Australia. On this occasion the underwear agents didn't get away with it. They were caught as they came into Britain through Customs and the ringleader was sent to jail. He also had to give up his notebook in which he had kept a record of all the smuggled birds and their owners, so it was possible to confiscate and rescue these birds as well.

There is a twist to this story that will give you something to think about. Remember that it has been illegal to export birds from Australia for forty years. This obviously means that Australian birds are very rare outside Australia, which makes them more valuable than ever to collectors. It also means that many of them are abundant inside Australia, so abundant in fact that they are sometimes destroyed as pests. Conservation issues rarely have straightforward solutions.

There is no doubt that people and parrots can get along very well together. Like dogs and horses, parrots are sociable animals that live in groups in the wild. A human parrot-owner is a poor substitute for a parrot companion but better than no companion at all. Luckily it is perfectly possible to buy cockatiels and budgerigars that have been bred in captivity for the pet trade. Budgies can live for thirty years or more if they are well cared for. If you have one, make sure you give it as good a life as possible. Parrots can live to a very ripe old age – old enough to get a bus pass! You can buy **commercially bred** parrots in this country. They are very expensive because breeding them is a specialised business. The parent parrots are usually kept in very small cages because, in captivity, many birds breed better in small enclosures than in large ones.

But wouldn't it be nicer to see them flying about in the wild? In some countries the money made from 'eco-tourists' – who want to see animals in their own habitats – helps pay towards preserving the natural habitat and wildlife.

Although the pet trade and rainforest destruction are the two main threats to parrots, one species of parrot may be saved by its captive relations. The Spix Macaw from Brazil was on the verge of extinction. As far as experts could tell, there was only one in existence in the wild. However, because of the bird trade, there were 39 in captivity around the world. With these it has been possible to set up a captive breeding programme to ensure the survival of the Spix for a while longer – but it mustn't be forgotten that it was the bird trade that caused its rarity in the first place.

Endangered birds can sometimes be helped by breeding programmes that are set up on their home ground. Five years ago, the Mauritius parakeet was the rarest parrot in the world. Its forest habitat was disappearing, making it more vulnerable than ever to its natural predators. Conservationists are now working with captive birds and wild ones together in the

forest to try and increase their numbers.
They are working in the same way with
kakapos in New Zealand. There are only 50
of these flightless parrots left and progress
with them is very slow. Kakapos are easy
prey for cats and dogs and stoats, all of
which have been introduced to New
Zealand comparatively recently in its history.

And so we come to parrots in zoos.
Parrots can be bred in safety in zoos with
the possibility of reintroducing them into
the wild if the numbers there ever get too
low. The Macaw Aviary at London Zoo
was built in 1994. What makes it special is
that it is very large. Wild parrots are
brilliant flyers – they fly high and fast – so it
really is a shame to house them in any
other way in captivity. Parrots are also
notorious for trashing any plants that grow
in their cage, so the aviary at the Zoo
contains special things for them to chew.
With plenty of birds and plenty of space,
the macaws are free to choose their own
mates, which is important when you pair

for life. Once they are breeding they can be aggressive towards the others, so breeding pairs are separated off into smaller aviaries.

Rearing parrots is skilled work. Recently Bird House staff had to look after two orphaned lory chicks. The baby black-winged lories (originally from small islands near New Guinea) were about the size of a little finger and had to be fed by hand all through the day from six in the morning until ten at night for nine weeks. Even experienced keepers find it hard to tell wild parrots apart at first, but hand-reared birds are different: they think their keepers are their parents (this is called imprinting) and follow them around. As they get older they sit on the keepers' shoulders and shout in their ears!

Parrots are marvellous birds. They belong in the tropical forests where there is room for them to fly in their huge colourful flocks. Many of them are at risk because their habitat is disappearing. It is sad that the other great threat they face comes from people wanting to own them. We don't want them to be loved to extinction.

MIX 'N' MATCH

Enclosures where there are more than one kind of animal are good for all the animals concerned – it is more stimulating for them to be with other species. Mixed enclosures also make for more interesting viewing. I stood for a long time in the October sunshine one afternoon watching the meerkats that live with the giraffes at London Zoo. The slow-moving, elegant giraffes are a great contrast to the speedy little meerkats that scamper along by the wall, stopping every now and then to stand up on their hind legs and act as lookouts. Lookups might be a better description! Even the two baby giraffes are more than three metres tall.

SOMETHING FISHY

Did you know that many seahorses mate
for life? And that every morning the couple
perform a little courtship dance in which
they link tails and change colour? Did you
even know that a seahorse was a fish?
Some people think that a seahorse is too
cute to be a fish, but in fact it's a close
relation of the pipefish, and a distant
relation of the common stickleback.

Perhaps the most extraordinary feature of
the seahorse, making it probably unique in
the animal world, is that the *males* get
pregnant. The female has an ovipositor (an
'egg-placer') through which she deposits
her eggs into a pouch on the male's tail.
The pouch seals up, the eggs embed
themselves into the wall of the pouch –
and grow. When the time comes, the male
will give birth – and the birth is not always
easy – to several hundred baby seahorses,

which will then swim off, tiny but fully formed and independent.

Seahorses are found all over the world in coastal waters, from the south coast of Britain to Tasmania, from **temperate** to tropical waters. They can be as small as a thumbnail or as long as your foot. They don't have scales like most fish but bony plates, and some have little spines, and all have a coronet on top of the head. They can change colour quickly to match the background and some have seaweedy **appendages** that look just like the real thing. Studies of one species showed that females move within a home range of about ten square metres, males of only about one square metre.

But there are facts about seahorses that are not so cute. Every year at least forty countries around the world are involved in the trade in millions of dried and live seahorses for traditional East Asian medicine alone. Hundreds of thousands more go to the tourist souvenir trade to become keyrings and bathroom ornaments. You might even have one yourself. But most of them, by far, end up in oriental health stores. You can buy them by the kilo, like flowerheads, for making a strength-giving tea, or you can buy them ground up into pills and potions which are used to cure everything from headaches to footrot. And while it's probable that some of these cures might work, it is also a fact that the world population of seahorses can't afford to lose so many a year.

This is where the conservationists, including the Zoological Society of London (ZSL), step in. But as you will see, saving seahorses is a very different matter from saving tigers and gorillas. Conservation is not simple.

One of the first puzzles for people working with seahorses is telling them apart. When they are alive they vary in size, change colour, sometimes have seaweedy bits, sometimes don't. Some have broader tummies or longer snouts than others, but even when scientists try to identify dried seahorses by taking at least *twenty-four* different measurements, it's still not always possible to identify the different types. **Genetic studies** of **DNA** will provide an accurate way to identify different seahorses, which can then be combined with the measurements, drawings and photographs of them, dead and alive, to provide an informative guide. Once they can be identified in this way, project-workers will be able to trace where they are sold and where they have come from so that they can target conservation efforts on the most important places and most threatened species.

The next problem lies in the fact that there is a high demand for seahorses, which makes them valuable, especially to the very poor people who catch them. In fact, the money they earn from catching seahorses might be their only means for keeping their families, especially in the Philippines, a Catholic country where families are large. This is a situation where conservationists want to make sure there are enough seahorses for everyone, rather than attempting to change centuries-old medicinal traditions.

Dr Amanda Vincent of McGill University, Canada, is passionate about seahorses. Together with ZSL, she runs Project Seahorse, a conservation programme for seahorses. Dr Vincent went to the Philippines, centre of seahorse fishery, to set up an important seahorse reserve in a village so remote it was one-and-a-half hour's walk and boat ride (no road, so no cars) from the nearest telephone! The Filippino Project Seahorse team work with the local community to understand the seahorse fishery and help with ways of conserving the wild seahorses, while allowing local people to make a living.

Heather Hall, Curator of the Reptile

House and Aquarium at the Zoo, made a visit there and spent a night out fishing with a local fisherman, as Project Seahorse team members often do. They set off at dusk in a wooden boat with a lantern and rowed out for an hour before jumping into the dark water where they would spend the next seven hours. Wearing simple goggles, a single wooden flipper, and carrying a spear, they dived to spear fish for food and to catch seahorses by hand to sell. Heather even fell asleep whilst snorkelling, the night was so long and gruelling. And that was a good night's fishing! The fisherman had enough fish to feed his family and eleven seahorses to sell.

The team has built a simple **field station** on stilts where water comes from a well and electricity for running the computers comes from solar panels in the roof. The villagers, who all live below the Filippino poverty line, have agreed that they need a **'sustainable** fishery'. So they have found a place on the reef to make a marine reserve, where fishing is prohibited. A boat patrols the area to make sure that no one cheats. And because no one is allowed to fish there, the amount of fish in the reserve has built up so much that they spill into the sea outside it. Now there are more fish than ever outside the reserve. It is such a good thing that other villages have asked for reserves in their area, where all sorts of fish as well as seahorses can thrive.

There are other ways to increase the numbers of seahorses: if a fisherman finds he has caught a pregnant male, he can now put it in a meshed-off area (a sea cage) until the babies have been born and swum off through the mesh. The poor old dad still cops it, but there are several hundred more babies than there would have been. There's also another cage to put young seahorses, where they can reproduce while growing to a more valuable size.

Project Seahorse is helping to increase the numbers of seahorses, at the same time improving the life of the villagers and also helping to save the vulnerable coastal areas – mangrove swamps, coral reefs, seagrass beds and estuaries – where seahorses are found. Conservationists might not like the fact that the seahorses end up as medicine, but they cannot deprive fishermen of their source of income – after all, other fish are caught to be eaten and nobody minds about that. But a worrying development in the medicine trade is that more people are buying ready-made pills made from ground up seahorses, rather than whole ones. This means that the quality of the seahorses themselves is less important than it was, so traders are less fussy about undersized ones.

Seahorses bound for the tourist souvenir trade are another matter. Nobody could claim to need earrings or ornaments made from seahorses. What's more, the fish, all taken from the wild, die being dried out on lines so that their tails curl. Project Seahorse asks you not to buy seahorses as souvenirs. They would also like to know where you saw seahorses for sale, what they cost and where they came from.

Some seahorses are sold as aquarium fish. Amateurs might not be aware that every seahorse on sale has in fact been caught in the wild. They are very difficult to keep because they need live food all year round, and many of them die after a couple of months. Then the owners buy another one, thinking perhaps that they are doing their bit for conservation if they manage to breed some. They aren't. That is best left to the professionals, and best of all, these fish should be left to live in the wild.

Zoos around the world have developed a captive breeding programme for seahorses. They swap information about how to keep and breed different species, so they don't need to be captured from the wild. Seahorses are not always on display at

London Zoo Aquarium as they get stressed when visitors constantly tap on the glass of their aquarium, and it's more important for the seahorses to be able to breed than for them to be on show to the public.

THE WORLD'S SMALLEST NATURE RESERVE

This is a story about snails. Before you read any further, here is an amazing fact about snails: there are more different species of snail than there are different species of all the vertebrates put together. Vertebrates – animals with backbones – such as mammals, birds, reptiles, amphibians, fish, make up only 3% of all animals. The other 97% are invertebrates, such as insects, spiders, and **molluscs** – which include snails. Snails! Those things that go crunch underfoot when it's been raining: in their own way they rule the world.

There are yet more interesting facts about snails: land-dwelling snails still need a lot of water so their bodies are slimy to prevent water from evaporating and their urine is solid, not liquid; they come out only when it's wet, and hibernate by digging themselves into the ground; snails are **hermaphrodites**, which means that they are both male and female, so when a pair mate, each snail fertilizes the other's eggs.

The *Partula* snails in this story live in the Polynesian islands of the Pacific. They look similar to any small snails but they are interesting for quite a few reasons. One is that they give birth to live young rather than eggs. Another is that they have a useful function in the rainforest 'web of life' because they feed on rotting plants, and quickly convert it to enrich the soil. The third reason has to do with **evolution**. *Partula* snails are tree snails that have lived for over a million years in the untouched rainforest of these paradise islands. There were no mammals, big reptiles or amphibians living on the islands so the snails had no enemies. Over a long period of time they evolved into many slightly different species, which makes them a great example of evolution at work. People have

been writing books about them for over
a century.

The Polynesian islanders also have a
centuries-old interest in these snails –
they make pretty necklaces from their
empty shells, as gifts and to sell.

So when, about twenty years ago, there
were suddenly far fewer *Partula* snails
around, a lot of people noticed. It was
humans – as so often – who were
responsible for their decline, but not in a
way you would imagine, because the villains
of the piece were in fact other snails.

During the 1960s, giant African land snails
were brought in to the islands. People eat
snails, and giant snails make bigger
mouthfuls. (Visit them in the Zoo – they
really are enormous.) It wasn't long before
some of these monsters escaped from the
snail farms and started munching their way
through the islanders' crops. The islanders
were not pleased. It's hard to get rid of

snails – ask any gardener. One way is to bring in yet more snails – **carnivorous** ones. So carnivorous snails called *Euglandina rosea* were brought in to eat the giant African ones. Unfortunately, the carnivorous snails preferred the little *Partula* snails. They made a more manageable snack than the giants, which were after all ten times their own size.

Within ten years several of the *Partula* species had become extinct. It was time for the conservationists to step in. Luckily, because of their interest to scientists, some *Partula* snails already existed in universities. More were rescued from the wild by expeditions to Polynesia. With all of these it was possible to set up a captive breeding programme. The snails bred in captivity could go back into the wild when it was safe for them again. London Zoo's Invertebrate Conservation Centre manages an international breeding programme that involves sixteen zoos and universities – and a major computer program.

The computer programme, CERCI, is a sort of **studbook** program for animals such as spiders and snails, where it's not possible to recognize an individual (as you can with tigers, for example). CERCI helps the scientists to put the right snails together, so that each species is kept separate, and only the right snails are mated together. It is an invaluable part of the captive breeding scheme. There are now *Partula* snails in zoos and universities all over the world. London Zoo alone has about 2000.

In 1993, some of the snails were released into the Palm House at Kew Gardens as an experiment. They settled in very happily and even started to breed. The time had come to set up the smallest **nature reserve** in the world.

In 1994, a team of scientists, including staff from London Zoo, set off to the Polynesian island of Moorea. Deep in the rainforest they built the little snail reserve. It measured twenty metres square. It even had a snail-sized electric fence and a barrier to keep out the carnivorous *Euglandina* snails. Three types of zoo-bred *Partula* snails were released, about 300 in all, 40 of them from London Zoo. The team collected more wild snails for the breeding programme from other islands before returning home.

There are 33 surviving species of *Partula*. Until New Year's Day in 1996 there were 34. On that day, the last of a *Partula* species called *turgida* died, extinct after 1.5 million years. But, because of the programme, scientists at least had the chance to study it before it disappeared for ever.

Meanwhile, all was not well at the reserve on Moorea. When a team returned there in 1996 they found that the electric fence was broken and *Euglandina* snails had got in. They mended the fence and released more captive-bred snails. Another visit later in the year showed that the *Euglandina* had got in again, though there were survivors of all three types of *Partula*. The fence and barrier were still proving a problem in 1997 – all because the fence was not being maintained properly. This time only one of the Partula species had survived the carnivorous invaders. The good news was that there were at least eleven of them and most of them were snails that had been born there on Moorea, not in a zoo.

So what happens next? The team hope to raise money for a student to go to Moorea and study the snails and also to keep watch over the reserve on a daily basis. They are looking at other islands, including Tahiti, for new reserves. The captive breeding programme flourishes with the help of CERCI and scientists can continue their evolutionary and **genetic studies** of these interesting snails. There is hope that one day all 33 of the remaining species of

Partula will be back where they belong in the islands doing their vital job of **recycling** plant material and enjoying their island home.

RING TALES

Ring-tailed coatis from South America are great little animals for encouraging children's interest at London Zoo Events. Unlike many of the animals at the Zoo their species is not in danger of imminent extinction. Could this be why they are so cheeky?

Not long ago three baby coatis had to be hand-reared at the Zoo. Events staff bottle-fed them day and night in their office. During this time other zoo staff found they were getting strange anonymous phone calls. It turned out that the little coatis had been pressing buttons on the office phone! They had to be moved to a phone-free zone before they ran up a big bill.

FUNKY GIBBONS

Which ones, precisely, are the gibbons? Are they monkeys or are they apes? What's the difference between monkeys and apes anyway? The simplest answer to that last question is that monkeys have tails and apes don't. There are the great apes (close relations of humans) – the chimpanzees, the orang-utans and the gorillas – and there are the lesser apes – the gibbons.

In the Zoo you will see big, slow-moving gorillas and cheeky chimps. The gibbons are the ones that swing elegantly from branch to branch on long arms with long hands, their feet barely touching the ground. Gibbons are the smallest apes, lightly built, with soft furry bodies.

Gibbons come from south-east Asia. They live in forests and spend all their time in the trees. Unlike many **primates**, they have a fairly limited diet of ripe fruit, which is harder to find than leaves and twigs. They live in small family groups, so that they are not competing with one another for food. The mother and father can sometimes stay together for life. They 'sing' every morning to warn other gibbons off their patch. Male and female sing their different songs as a duet. This can be one of the loudest sounds in the Zoo first thing in the morning – quite a dawn chorus!

The mother gibbon has one baby every two or three years – it quickly learns how to cling on to her fur as she swings through the branches. The children start to mature at around seven or eight years old and reach adulthood at about nine. Then they go off to start their own families.

Gibbons do not make good pets, and yet the pet trade is one of the main reasons they are endangered. Cute baby ones are on sale in many markets in south-east Asia, all captured from the wild. It's hard to housetrain an animal that normally lives in the trees, and however sweet gibbons are as babies they soon become jealous and aggressive, especially if they have to share their owner with a partner or children. So most of them end up being passed on to overcrowded animal 'orphanages' after a few years or even a few months. Because gibbons are endangered, zoos are sometimes able to house rescued **pure-bred** males and females for their captive breeding programmes. (They're very seldom taken from the wild any more.) But there are many reasons why these pet gibbons may not be suitable for a breeding programme. One might never have had the company of other gibbons, another might not be the appropriate variety and it would be illegal anyway to export it out of its native country. There are even more reasons why pet gibbons cannot be returned to the wild. Usually it's because their bit of 'wild' no longer exists. Even if it did, the pet gibbon would be unable to find food without upsetting the gibbon family groups that are already living there. So it's not surprising the 'orphanages' are overcrowded.

Some of the rarest and most threatened gibbons are the white-cheeked gibbons from south-east China, Laos, Vietnam, and parts of Kampuchea. White-cheeked gibbons are born golden brown. As they get older both males and females turn black with a crest and white cheeks. But then, once they reach adulthood, the females change again, turning golden brown with a black crest. The males stay black. Remember this. It is important to the story of Concy the white-cheeked gibbon.

Concy was bought as a pet from a market in Bangkok (Thailand) and taken home to Jordan, in the Middle East, by the new owner. As you might expect, at around five years old, Concy had started to become vicious and the owners appealed to the Royal Society for the Conservation of

Nature in Jordan for help. They rang a
gibbon rescue centre in Thailand who
suggested that London Zoo might be
interested in this particular white-cheeked
gibbon. They were right. London Zoo did
want to rescue a healthy male for the
European breeding programme of these
highly endangered gibbons, and since there
were no legal problems about exporting
Concy from Jordan, a flight was booked.
And not a regular flight! Queen Nour of
Jordan supported the move and Concy had
a free flight with Royal Jordanian Airways.
The white-cheeked gibbon duly arrived in a
beautiful box, sedated, and wearing a
nappy. The official papers described it as a
nine-year-old male. The Zoo had no reason
to believe otherwise.

New arrivals to the Zoo usually undergo a
thorough health check under anaesthetic,
straight away, but Concy needed some
time to settle in, so it was decided to put
off the health check until the end of the
six-month **quarantine** period. But it

wasn't long before that nappy dropped off and – shock, horror! It appeared that the male gibbon destined to be the new founder of the breeding programme had been neutered. What a disaster! But the Zoo staff decided not to panic. All would become clear when it was time for the health check. Until then they had to be content with the possibility that Concy was still immature and undeveloped.

Another possibility was that Concy was a female considerably younger than nine years, and therefore still black in colour. That possibility became a probability as Concy's fur obligingly started to turn golden during the next few weeks. When the health check finally took place it was confirmed that she was indeed a female white-cheeked gibbon.

But the problems didn't stop there. A male called Tot was flown in from France to be Concy's mate. Tot had been taken from the wild to a zoo in eastern Europe before eventually ending up in a French zoo. His health check had another shock in store. He had hepatitis and had to go into quarantine. Concy had to be inoculated, and so did all the zoo staff who worked with the gibbons.

Incidentally, if, like me, you imagined the keepers having all sorts of fun and games with the gibbons, you'd be quite wrong. Gibbons are aggressive to anyone outside their family group and their huge teeth can be savage. Head keeper, Mick Carman, surprised me by saying of the male gibbon as he swung over to us (fortunately on the other side of the fence), "That one's threatening me!" In fact, the male was just being very protective of Concy, and that makes him aggressive towards his keepers.

Once Tot was out of quarantine there remained a final huge bridge to be crossed. Would the pair take to each other? After all, both the gibbons had different backgrounds and Concy had spent most of her life with humans. What a waste it would be if, after all that trouble, the pair didn't get on and had to be separated. Their introduction was a dramatic moment. Everyone's hearts were in their mouths. Imagine their delight when Tot and Concy immediately hugged each other! The next phase of the European breeding programme could begin.

TURTLE DIARY

Big turtles can live to be a hundred, and like all reptiles, they keep on growing. So what is a zoo to do, when they outgrow their aquarium?

It's easy to declare that they shouldn't be there in the first place because turtles should surely do their turtle thing in the wide open seas, but the turtles in this story were in fact rescued from a fate far worse than living in a small aquarium in a zoo. One had been found dying in a pet shop before it was bought and taken to the Zoo in 1984. The other two were **customs seizures** in 1986 and 1989, one bound for a pet shop in someone's luggage, the other in a shipment of tropical fish.

All three hawksbill turtles were about 30cm long when they first arrived at London Zoo. There were two males and

one female. One of the males had a
damaged flipper, which was how he could
be recognised from the other male. The
Zoo's aquarium gave them enough room to
recover and flourish. But it soon became
apparent that the turtles were going to
outgrow it before too long. By now they
were nearly a metre in length.

It would have been very satisfying to tip
them back in the sea and wave goodbye,
knowing that they would live the next
ninety years in comfort, but sadly that was
not possible. Hawksbill turtles are found
across a wide range in tropical seas. They
migrate huge distances, but they always
miraculously return to their own nesting
beach. No one knew which three different
places these turtles had started from, and
it was more likely, with their turbulent
childhoods, that they would no longer
know where they had to get back to. They
would be in danger from hunters who
catch hawksbill turtles to use for 'tortoise-
shell'. To complicate matters further, as

long-term captives they could be carrying some disease which might in turn infect the wild turtles.

So returning them to the wild wasn't an option. Nor was finding them another zoo or aquarium in Britain or Europe – no one had space in a big enough aquarium. But there was space at Sea World in Florida, where they were building a new enclosure outdoors with nesting beaches, deep pools, shallow pools . . . and Sea World was keen to offer the hawksbill turtles a home.

It took three years to complete all the formalities that are necessary when animals with unknown backgrounds are transported across the world, but eventually the hawksbill turtles were cleared to go. Next problem: how do you go about transporting three gigantic marine animals from London to Florida? Not in your luggage, that's for sure!

Experts at Southampton University

recommended flying the turtles out in a 'combi', a combined cargo and passenger plane where passengers can have access to the cargo during the flight. The nearest airport for these special planes is in Paris. So the turtles had first to be transported there. Eurostar was out of the question, but the ferry was fine, providing a five-seater vehicle with room for three turtle boxes could be found. You don't see these every day, but a minibus with some of the seats removed proved to be the ideal turtle-mobile. The turtle boxes were large, rope-handled, wooden crates lined with foam rubber that could be soaked and kept wet throughout the journey.

At last all the details were worked out and the turtles and five staff members from London Zoo and Sea World – including a vet – were on their way to Florida. The press were all there to say goodbye, including Carlton TV's 'London Tonight' which was broadcast from the Zoo that evening as a special farewell.

Once out of quarantine, the turtles were released into their new enclosure at Sea World. After one week the staff at London Zoo received a fax from Sea World to let them know that the three had settled in very well. One male takes a walk on the beach in the sunshine every evening! Children come to Turtle Point at Sea World to see the turtles and learn about them.

The hawksbill turtles have gone from a tank at London Zoo that held 7000 gallons to one containing 70,000 gallons – with beaches – at Sea World. It's not the sea, but it must be the next best thing.

WISE OLD BIRD

Josephine the Great Indian Hornbill is the oldest bird in the Zoo. She has lived there since 1951 – and seen all sorts of changes. In 1951, not many people had television and even then the picture was black and white, so a zoo was the only place where you could see wild animals from other parts of the world.

Nearly half a century later, Josephine is living in a zoo which has become a conservation centre where endangered animals are bred – not all the animals are even on show to the public. Visitors of all ages come to learn more about animals so that they can be aware of conservation issues and the importance of 'biodiversity' – the wide range of different animals on the planet.

THE CONTINUING SAGA OF HARI

Imagine being able to drive home with a newborn tiger cub to look after! One of the keepers at London Zoo, Caroline Connor, became the lucky 'mother' to Hari the Sumatran tiger cub, cuddling him, playing with him and, of course, bottle-feeding him all hours of the day and night during the first weeks of his life. Animals at London Zoo are only hand-reared if they would die otherwise, but looking after Hari was just a tiny part of a worldwide operation to save the tiger from extinction.

There are five different sorts of tiger: Indian, Amur (also known as Siberian), Sumatran, Indo-Chinese and South China. All of them are at risk from changes to their habitat – and hunters. Perhaps one of the greatest threats to the tiger is its importance in traditional East Asian medicine, where every part of its body is considered to have healing properties. This means that poachers can make a lot of money by shooting tigers and selling them. The South China tiger is on the verge of extinction and the Sumatran tiger, like Hari, numbers no more than 600 in the wild. The international effort needed to protect tigers is enormous, and zoos all over the world are taking part in the conservation programme.

You know that conservation means protecting wild animals and their habitats. It also means educating people about endangered animals, particularly in the countries where those animals live. It means swapping information about rare animals. It means raising as much money as possible to fund that education and research. Then there is the captive breeding of endangered species, which is where zoos come in.

European zoos have taken responsibilty for

breeding Sumatran tigers. The number of tigers being bred has to be carefully regulated. There should be enough *unrelated* pure-bred males and females to produce healthy cubs in the future, but there mustn't be too many to go round the zoos that hold them. To make this possible, details of every single tiger going back over 30 years are held in a 'studbook' – a computer database which is coordinated at London Zoo by Sarah Christie. She makes sure that there are roughly 10 litters a year born throughout 45 zoos, and recommends precisely which animals should have cubs together.

For many years London Zoo kept tigers. They didn't need to breed them and produce more tigers, so the females were given a tiger variation of the contraceptive pill to stop them having babies. The male tiger, Martin, was one of very few pure-bred Sumatran and it became important that he should father cubs. The computer came up with Mira from Bremerhaven Zoo, in Germany, as the ideal mate and she was flown over to London to be with him.

Martin and Mira got on like a house on fire, but sadly Mira's first few cubs all died. Staff at the Zoo try not to interfere with a mother and her cubs if at all possible, but by now her keepers knew that, as a hand-reared tiger herself, Mira might have no idea how to care for her own cubs. They would have to keep a close eye on her if the latest cub or cubs were to survive.

When you were a baby your parents probably listened in on you with a baby alarm. That's just what the keepers set up in their mess-room to listen for the first mews of a new cub that would let them know that Mira had given birth. Then, better still, they were offered close-circuit TV so that they could see the cubbing den on monitors in the mess-room without disturbing Mira. Imagine their excitement when early one January morning they were able to watch the cub being born!

At first all was well, but soon the keepers could see that Mira didn't know how to look after her cub. She kept picking it up and moving it around, and she wouldn't allow it to feed from her. Because Mira was still responsive to her keepers, they were able to lure her away so they could have a good look at her baby. That's when they saw that she had already managed to injure it. So the keepers made the difficult decision to take the cub away from its mother and feed it on milk from a bottle instead. It meant two-hourly feeds, day and night, but it was the only way the rare Sumatran tiger cub would stay alive.

As with all new babies, the cub needed one main mother – and that was Caroline's job for the first three weeks of his life. Later, all the staff took their turns to babysit. Sometimes the little tiger seemed almost too popular, and the mess-room where he had his nursery became overcrowded with admiring visitors from all sections of the Zoo. Soon monitors were set up outside, so the public could see him too. When he became too big to travel to and from Caroline's home in her car, he was put in a nursery in a glass-fronted show den. By now the cub had a name, Hari, after a river in Sumatra. (The competition to name him was won by 8-year-old Alexander Smith.) In three months Hari had grown from 1.1kg to 13.5kg. His daily diet consisted of 300ml of milk, a 1kg joint of meat, 500g of mince and an egg.

If Hari wasn't to become too humanised, he needed an animal playmate as well as his human ones. Puppies make good playmates for big kittens. It had to be the right sort of puppy and it needed an owner to give it a permanent home. One of the Zoo drivers found the perfect puppy — a Japanese Akita called Liffey — for Esther Wenman, Head Keeper of Reptiles. For a while, Esther looked after the puppy whilst one of the Lion House staff looked after the cub, both in the tiger nursery. They both needed lots of exercise, so they were taken out for walks together. Hari and Liffey became excellent friends. They played together for six months, giving Hari a good chance to socialise with another animal, all part of his real tiger education. But of course as Hari grew bigger and bigger, the time came for Liffey to go back to being an ordinary pet dog. Now Liffey's only unusual behaviour is that she never asks you to play like a normal dog, but waits, cat-like, for you to play with her!

Big Hari still played at rough and tumble with his keepers. He loved to jump up and hug them. The keepers got through uniforms very quickly, and soon discovered that firefighter's jackets (Caroline's father is a firefighter) gave much better protection against accidental scratches. Like all kittens, Hari couldn't retract his claws at first, though he always played with sheathed claws later. But then it was time for him to meet some real tigers. As it happened, two Siberian – or Amur – tiger cubs were on their way from Moscow to Britain, bound for Whipsnade Wild Animal Park and Edinburgh Zoo. Sarah Christie persuaded the zoos to allow the Amur cubs to spend their quarantine time at London Zoo. That way they could be companions for Hari for a few months before going on to their new homes. The hours spent playing with Liffey had taught Hari how to play with other animals and the three tigers got on well together. So Hari finally learned to become a real tiger.

After 34 years at the Zoo, ten of them with big cats, Head Keeper Ray Charter knows that you can never trust a big cat one hundred per cent. They are 'predictably unpredictable' – and that is how a tiger should be. Sheer size and weight are a problem if a tiger becomes too boisterous, even if its claws are sheathed. The keepers could see that it was getting towards the end of their own glorious friendship with Hari when he began to push his luck with them. A wild tiger will always want to dominate.

Hari's parents, Martin and Mira, went their separate ways. Mira went back to Germany and Martin went to Chessington World of Adventure, where a neutered female has been found to keep him company. And now Hari has also gone off, to the South Lakes Wildlife Park, to be a dad. A new female, Raika, has arrived at London Zoo, and a suitable mate is being found for her. With luck, Raika will not have the same problems with her cubs as Mira. By the time you read this book there might even be a new cub for you to visit at London Zoo, or the South Lakes Wildlife Park . . .

GLOSSARY

The glossary gives an explanation of some unusual words and expressions that are used in this book.

arachnophobia
fear of spiders

appendages
attachments (arms, legs, tails, or parts that look like these)

behavioural enrichment
making life more interesting for captive animals

biodiversity
the existence of a wide range of plants and animals in a particular habitat

captive breeding
breeding animals in an enclosed place to ensure their survival

carnivorous
meat-eating

CITES
Convention on International Trade in
Endangered Species

commercially bred
bred in captivity for sale

conservation
saving plants, animals and their habitats for
future generations

customs seizure
an illegal animal (or other object) that has
been seized by Customs when someone is
trying to smuggle it in to a country

DNA
the material which makes up the genetic
'recipe' for all living organisms

diet
what a particular animal eats

endangered
in danger of dying out

evolution
the gradual development and adaptation of
living things to suit a particular way of life

export
send abroad

extinct
when there are no more of a particular
plant or animal species left alive

field station
laboratory or study area built in or near
the wild

genetic studies
studies on the DNA of plants and animals.
Each living being has its own genetic recipe
in their DNA, but related plants and
animals have many parts of their recipes
that match, so genetic studies can give
useful information on relationships

between plants and animals.

habitat
the natural home of a plant or animal, and everything that it includes

hand-rearing
when a baby animal is fed and raised by humans rather than its mother

hermaphrodite
animal that has both male and female reproductive parts

hibernate
to sleep through the winter

invertebrates
animals without backbones (eg insects)

molluscs
animals such as snails and shellfish – also octopuses

moulting
losing and replacing an outer covering,
such as fur or feathers or sometimes the
whole skin

nature reserve
area on land or sea where animals and
plants are protected

nocturnal
active at night

pedipalps
pincer-like feelers on spiders, crabs etc

primates
mammals such as apes, monkeys, also
humans

protected species
animals that are protected by law. If you
are caught disturbing them you will have to
pay a fine or go to prison

pure-bred
not crossed with another sub-species

quarantine
isolation of an animal, especially one
that has just arrived from somewhere
else, to prevent the spread of infectious
diseases, particularly rabies

rainforests
forests in the hot, wet areas near the
Equator that are home to a huge variety of
plants and animals

recycling
reusing, often for a different purpose

red list
list of the species most at risk of extinction

reintroduce
putting captive-bred animals back into
the wild

simulation program
computer program that is used to make
predictions from facts

species
a group of animals (or plants) that are like
each other and can reproduce together

studbook
a record of all the known animals of a
particular species held in captivity

sustainable
where there are enough of a plant
or animal species to reproduce
themselves and maintain their numbers

tagged
when an animal has been marked,
sometimes electronically, so that you can
follow its movements and/or identify
an individual

temperate
neither very cold nor very hot – Britain

has a temperate climate

tropical
hot – near the Equator

web of life
a group of plants and animals that all
depend on the others being there

USEFUL ADDRESSES

London Zoo
Regent's Park
London
NW1 4RY

The Zoological Society of London
Regent's Park
London
NW1 4RY

The following are all mentioned in the book and are worth visiting if you're in the area.

Chessington World of Adventures
Leatherhead Road
Chessington
Surrey
KT9 2 NE

Chester Zoo
Caughall Road
Upton-by-Chester
Cheshire
CH2 1LH

South Lakes Wild Animal Park
Crossgates
Dalton-in-Furness
Cumbria
LA15 8JR

Whipsnade Wild Animal Park
Dunstable
Bedfordshire
LU6 2LF

LIFEWATCH

How you can help London Zoo's conservation work:

- Join Lifewatch, London Zoo's membership scheme, and you'll be helping to fund captive breeding work with some of the world's most endangered animals. Lifewatch members get free admission to London Zoo for one year.

- Knock spots off other gifts – adopt an animal for a friend! You can adopt any animal at London Zoo; species range from a seahorse to an elephant. Of course, you could always treat yourself to an animal adoption, too, or ask for one for a birthday present . . .

For more information, write to:

Lifewatch & Adoptions
London Zoo
Regent's Park
London
NW1 4RY

or telephone
0171 449 6262

111

VOUCHER FOR LONDON ZOO ADMISSION

LONDON ZOO ™

CONSERVATION IN ACTION

This voucher admits ONE CHILD FREE when accompanied by a full-paying adult.

A child is aged 4 to 14 inclusive.
Valid until 30 April 1999.
Not to be used in conjunction with any other offer.

Open every day except Christmas Day from 10am.

Nearest tube, Camden Town or Bus 274 from Baker Street or Oxford Street (Selfridges end).

London Zoo, Regent's Park, London NW1 4RY
Telephone 0171 722 3333

Hodder
Children's
Books

SAVING THE ANIMALS BY KATE PETTY